MASERATI
GRANTURISMO
BY EMILY ROSE OACHS

BELLWETHER MEDIA • MINNEAPOLIS, MN

Are you ready to take it to the extreme? Torque books thrust you into the action-packed world of sports, vehicles, mystery, and adventure. These books may include dirt, smoke, fire, and dangerous stunts.

WARNING: read at your own risk.

This edition first published in 2018 by Bellwether Media, Inc.

No part of this publication may be reproduced in whole or in part without written permission of the publisher. For information regarding permission, write to Bellwether Media, Inc., Attention: Permissions Department, 5357 Penn Avenue South, Minneapolis, MN 55419.

Library of Congress Cataloging-in-Publication Data

Names: Oachs, Emily Rose, author.
Title: Maserati GranTurismo / by Emily Rose Oachs.
Description: Minneapolis, MN : Bellwether Media, Inc., 2018. | Series:
   Torque: Car Crazy | Includes bibliographical references and index. |
   Audience: Ages 7-12.
Identifiers: LCCN 2017031294 (print) | LCCN 2017032233 (ebook) | ISBN 9781626177789
   (hardcover : alk. paper) | ISBN 9781681034836 (ebook)
Subjects: LCSH: Maserati GranTurismo automobile–Juvenile literature.
Classification: LCC TL215.M34 (ebook) | LCC TL215.M34 O23 2018 (print) | DDC
   629.222/2--dc23
LC record available at https://lccn.loc.gov/2017031294

Text copyright © 2018 by Bellwether Media, Inc. TORQUE and associated logos are trademarks and/or registered trademarks of Bellwether Media, Inc. SCHOLASTIC, CHILDREN'S PRESS, and associated logos are trademarks and/or registered trademarks of Scholastic Inc., 557 Broadway, New York, NY 10012.

Editor: Betsy Rathburn   Designer: Josh Brink

Printed in the United States of America, North Mankato, MN.

TABLE OF CONTENTS

TRAVEL IN COMFORT	4
THE HISTORY OF MASERATI	8
MASERATI GRANTURISMO	12
TECHNOLOGY AND GEAR	14
TODAY AND THE FUTURE	20
GLOSSARY	22
TO LEARN MORE	23
INDEX	24

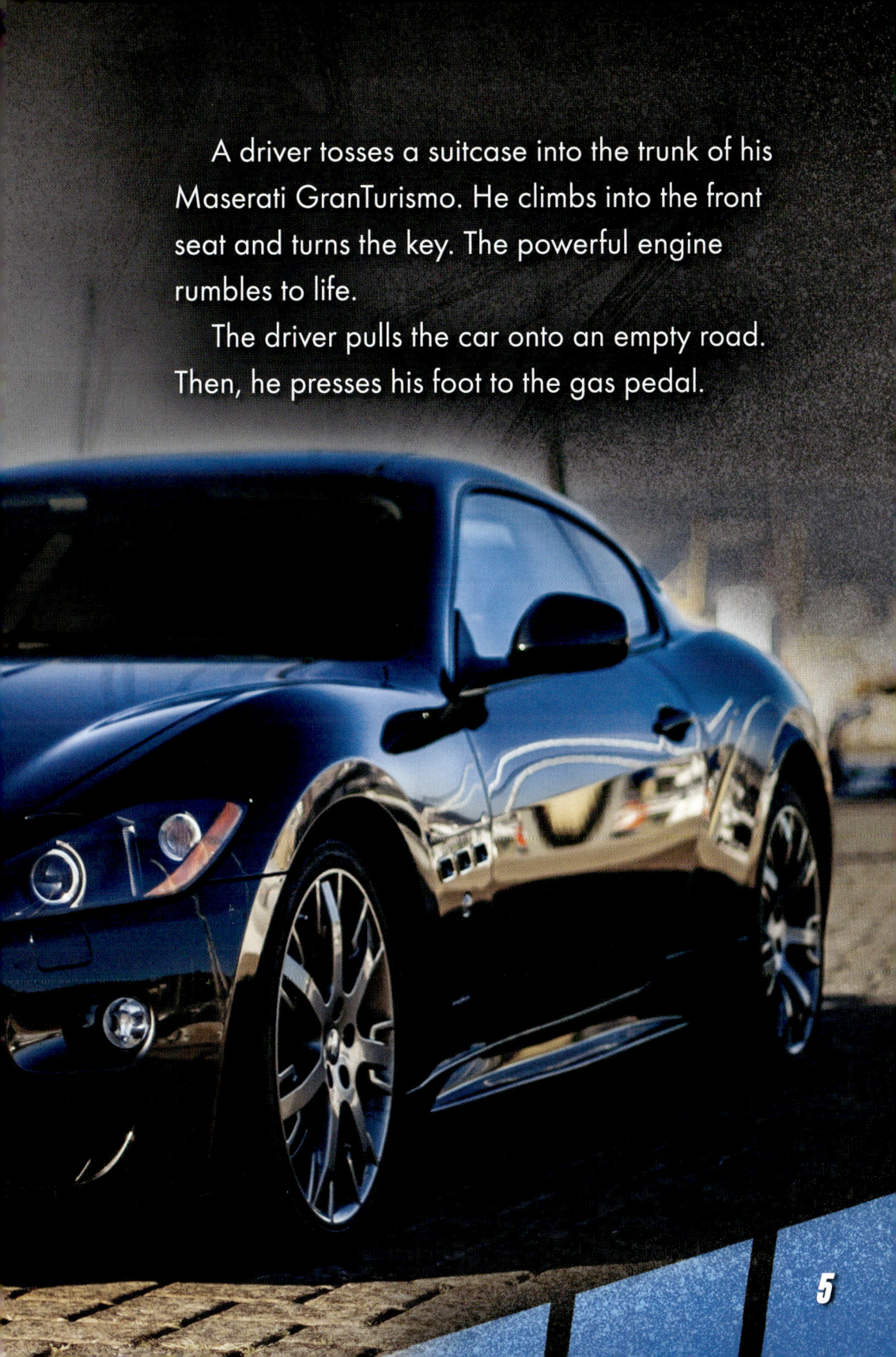

A driver tosses a suitcase into the trunk of his Maserati GranTurismo. He climbs into the front seat and turns the key. The powerful engine rumbles to life.

The driver pulls the car onto an empty road. Then, he presses his foot to the gas pedal.

The driver takes the Maserati GranTurismo down busy city streets. Then, he crosses into the countryside. In seconds, the car speeds past 60 miles (97 kilometers) per hour.

The GranTurismo handles the wide turns easily as it winds around green hills. The driver relaxes into his comfortable leather seat. His trip is just beginning.

THE HISTORY OF MASERATI

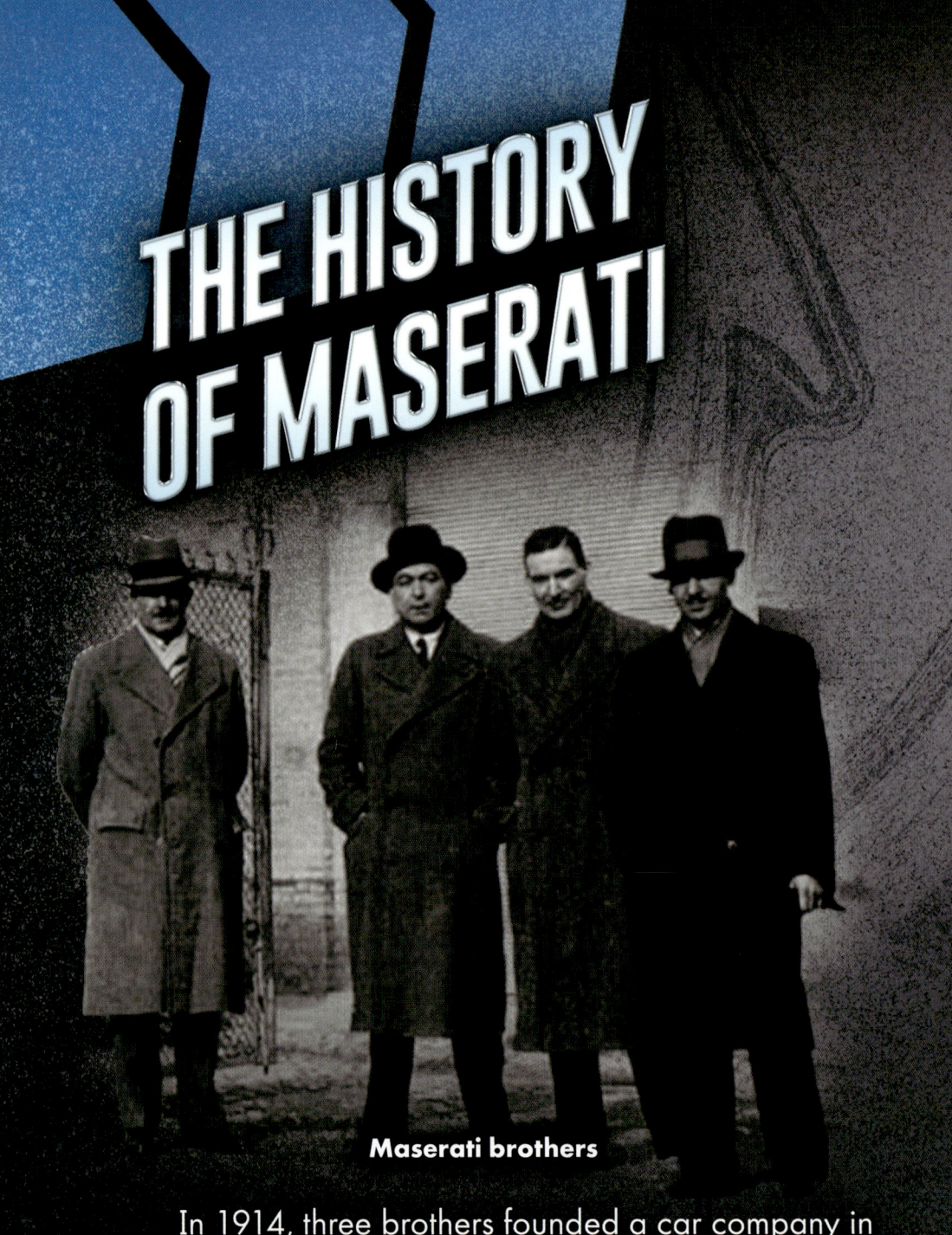

Maserati brothers

In 1914, three brothers founded a car company in Bologna, Italy. At first, the company made car parts. But it completed the first Maserati car in 1926.

The first car marked the start of a long racing history. Maserati vehicles became **Grand Prix** champions in Europe. In 1937, the brothers sold the company to a man named Adolfo Orsi.

1926 Maserati Tipo 26 B

SEA INSPIRATION

A FOURTH MASERATI BROTHER DESIGNED THE COMPANY'S FAMOUS TRIDENT LOGO. HIS INSPIRATION CAME FROM A STATUE OF THE ROMAN SEA GOD, NEPTUNE.

Adolfo kept improving Maserati cars. They raced to victory in early **Formula One** events. Adolfo also started designing Maserati vehicles for everyday driving. He brought **luxury** to sporty race cars.

Maserati 250F race car

Maserati MC12

In 1993, a carmaker called Fiat purchased the company. Since then, Maserati has continued to make speedy cars famous for their comfort!

MASERATI GRANTURISMO

The Maserati GranTurismo made its **debut** at the 2007 Geneva Motor Show. It came out about 60 years after Maserati introduced its first road car. The GranTurismo wowed crowds with its powerful engine.

2007 Maserati GranTurismo

HAPPY BIRTHDAY CAR

IN 2014, MASERATI INTRODUCED THE GRANTURISMO MC STRADALE CENTENNIAL EDITION. THIS SPORTY CAR WAS RELEASED TO CELEBRATE MASERATI'S 100TH YEAR IN BUSINESS!

2015 Maserati GranTurismo MC Stradale Centennial Edition

Later, Maserati replaced the original GranTurismo with improved versions. The Sport and MC **models** bring greater luxury and power to the GranTurismo lineup.

TECHNOLOGY AND GEAR

Maserati designed the GranTurismo with performance and style in mind. The newest versions can race to 185 miles (298 kilometers) per hour. Strong brakes help drivers stay in control.

Sleek lines make the car more **aerodynamic**. A **rear diffuser** and **side skirts** help it move even more quickly.

side skirt

POWER COLOR
RED HIGHLIGHTS DECORATE THE TRIDENT ON THE FRONT GRILLE. MASERATI ONLY ADDS THIS DETAIL TO ITS CARS WITH THE GREATEST POWER!

Cars in the GranTurismo lineup come as either **convertibles** or **coupes**. Owners pick from a wide range of paint colors and other options.

coupe

convertible

bolster →

Inside, two rows of leather seats allow four people to ride in comfort. Sporty side **bolsters** support the driver and passengers on tight turns.

Control lies at the driver's fingertips. Stereo buttons on the steering wheel are lined with chrome. Nearby **paddle shifters** help drivers easily switch gears.

Each GranTurismo comes with a Sport button. This button adjusts the car's gear changes and **suspension**. This boosts the car's performance.

paddle shifter

2017 MASERATI GRANTURISMO SPORT SPECIFICATIONS

CAR STYLE	COUPE OR CONVERTIBLE
ENGINE	4.7L V8
TOP SPEED	185 MILES (298 KILOMETERS) PER HOUR
0 - 60 TIME	4.7 SECONDS
HORSEPOWER	454 HP (338.5 KILOWATTS) @ 7,100 RPM
CURB WEIGHT	4,350 POUNDS (1,973 KILOGRAMS)
WIDTH	81 INCHES (205.7 CENTIMETERS)
LENGTH	194.2 INCHES (493.3 CENTIMETERS)
HEIGHT	53.3 INCHES (135.4 CENTIMETERS)
WHEEL SIZE	20 INCHES (50.8 CENTIMETERS)
COST	STARTS AT $132,825

TODAY AND THE FUTURE

The GranTurismo has been popular since its introduction. More than 40,000 have been sold!

New designs for the next **generation** of the GranTurismo are already underway. Like earlier versions, the new GranTurismo will stay true to Maserati's racing roots!

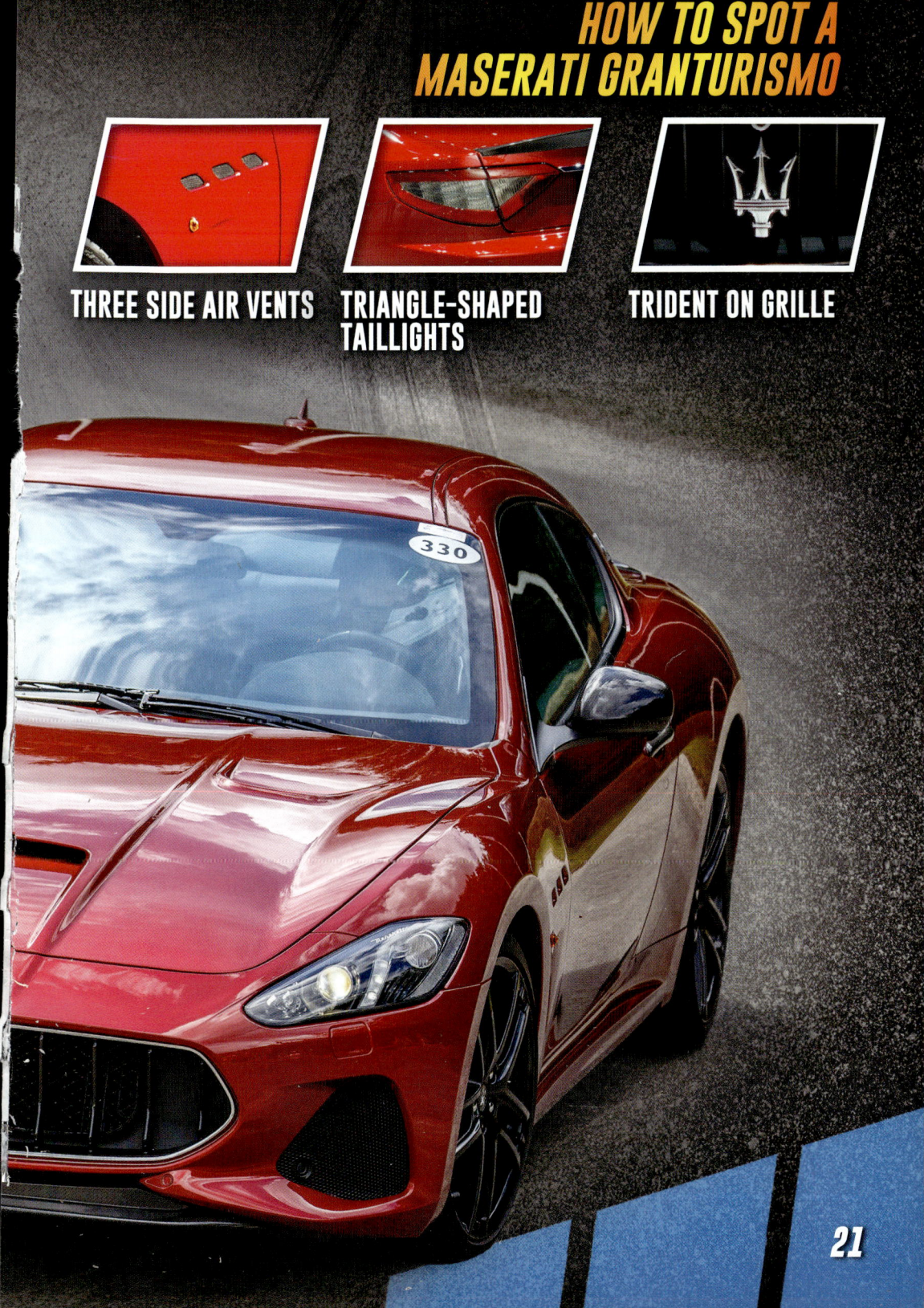

GLOSSARY

aerodynamic—having a shape that can move through the air quickly

bolsters—cushions on either side of a seat

convertibles—cars with folding or soft roofs

coupes—cars with hard roofs and two doors

debut—a first-time introduction

Formula One—a type of car racing

generation—a version of the same model

Grand Prix—a high-level racing competition

luxury—expensive and offering great comfort

models—specific kinds of cars

paddle shifters—paddles on the steering wheel of a car that allow a driver to change gears

rear diffuser—a part on the back underside of a car that directs air and makes the car more aerodynamic

side skirts—lips on the sides of a car's body that make the car more aerodynamic

suspension—a car's system of springs and shocks that help a car grip the road

TO LEARN MORE

AT THE LIBRARY

Baker, Theo. *Maserati Gran Turismo*. Vero Beach, Fla.: Rourke Educational Media, 2017.

Gray, Leon. *Fast and Cool Cars*. New York, N.Y.: DK, Penguin Random House, 2015.

Kenney, Karen Latchana. *Thrilling Sports Cars*. North Mankato, Minn.: Capstone Press, 2015.

ON THE WEB

Learning more about the Maserati GranTurismo is as easy as 1, 2, 3.

1. Go to www.factsurfer.com.

2. Enter "Maserati GranTurismo" into the search box.

3. Click the "Surf" button and you will see a list of related web sites.

With factsurfer.com, finding more information is just a click away.

INDEX

aerodynamic, 14

body, 16

Bologna, Italy, 8

bolsters, 17

brakes, 14

colors, 15, 16

comfort, 6, 11, 17

company, 8, 9, 10, 11, 12, 13, 14, 15, 20

design, 9, 10, 14, 20

engine, 5, 12

Europe, 9

Fiat, 11

Formula One, 10

generation, 20

Geneva Motor Show, 12

Grand Prix, 9

handling, 6

history, 8, 9, 10, 11, 12, 13

how to spot, 21

interior, 17, 18

Maserati brothers, 8, 9

models, 10, 11, 13, 14

Orsi, Adolfo, 9, 10

paddle shifters, 18

racing, 9, 10, 20

rear diffuser, 14

sales, 20

side skirts, 14

specifications, 19

speed, 6, 11, 14

Sport button, 18

suspension, 18

trident logo, 9, 15, 21

The images in this book are reproduced through the courtesy of: Stefan Ataman, front cover; gyn9037, pp. 2-3; Clari Massimiliano, pp. 4-5, 6-7; Bkise001/ Wikipedia, p. 8; Eric Vandeville/ Getty Images, p. 9 (top); Faiz Zak, p. 9 (bottom); Motoring Picture Library/ Alamy, p. 10; dimcars, p. 11; Hans Dieter Seufert/ Alamy, p. 12; VanderWolfImages, p. 13; Dong liu, pp. 14, 19; Chris Willson/ Alamy, p. 15; Roman.S-Photographer, p. 16; Mirage_studio, p. 16 (bottom); eVox/ Alamy, p. 17; Kimball Stock Collection, p. 18; pbpgalleries/ Alamy, pp. 20-21; Philip Pilosian, p. 21 (top left); betto rodrigues, p. 21 (top middle); Darren Brode, p. 21 (top right).

629.222 O FLT
Oachs, Emily Rose,
Maserati GranTurismo /

06/18

Friends of the
Houston Public Library